Knowledge Books and Software

No matter where you go in Australia, you will find towns and cities with Aboriginal meanings. One of our most important cities is our capital city, Canberra. Did you know that it means "**meeting place**" in the Ngunnawal language?

Knowledge Books and Software

Wagga Wagga is a city in western NSW. It is home to the Wiradjuri people. It means "**land of many crows**".

Knowledge Books and Software

5

Gunnedah is home to the Kamilaroi people in western NSW and means "**place of white stones**". Today, you can find sheep stations in the area.

Knowledge Books and Software

7

The Gold Coast in Queensland has many Aboriginal suburb names. Tallebudgera is one of them and home to the Yugambeh people. It means "**good fish**".

Knowledge Books and Software

9

In Western Queensland, you can find the small town of Biloela. The Gangulu people called it Biloela after the **white cockatoo** which was their totem. You can still find many white cockatoos there today.

Knowledge Books and Software

11

Ballarat, in Victoria, is the traditional home of the Wadawurrung people. It means "**resting place**". Ballarat has become a very busy town since the start of the Gold Rush.

Knowledge Books and Software

Legana, in Tasmania, means "**fresh water**" in the local palawa kani language. Legana is on the Tamar River at the spot where the river becomes fresh water.

Knowledge Books and Software

Coober Pedy, in South Australia, is famous for its underground homes, called dugouts. The name was taken from local Aboriginal words which mean **"white man in a hole"**.

Knowledge Books and Software

Western Australia is a very large, dry state. You can find Meekatharra almost in the middle. This Yamatji word means "**place of little water**".

Knowledge Books and Software

19

Over 1000 km away on the coast, you can find Ningaloo. This means **"deep water"** for the local Yinigudura people. People travel here from all over the country to swim with the whale sharks.

Knowledge Books and Software

21

Mataranka in the Northern Territory is a very popular tourist spot. It means "**place of the snake**" in Yangman language. Australia is a vast country, and our First Nations languages can be found in many different place names, so start exploring today!

Knowledge Books and Software

23

Word bank

Australia

Aboriginal

Canberra

language

Wagga Wagga

Wiradjuri

Gunnedah

Kamilaroi

Tallebudgera

Yugambeh

Biloela

cockatoo

Ballarat

traditional

Legana

Tasmania

palawa kani

Coober Pedy

underground

dugouts

Meekatharra

Ningaloo

Mataranka

Knowledge Books and Software